J 623.825
Bodde
Bodden, Valerie

Battleships

1

10/30/20

Keep this card in the book pocket
Book is due on the latest date stamped

BUILT *for* BATTLE

BATTLESHIPS

Valerie Bodden

CREATIVE ◆ EDUCATION

Published by Creative Education
P.O. Box 227, Mankato, Minnesota 56002
Creative Education is an imprint of The Creative Company
www.thecreativecompany.us

Design and production by Liddy Walseth
Art direction by Rita Marshall
Printed by Corporate Graphics in the United States of America

Photographs by Corbis (Bettmann), DefenseImagery (Don S. Montgomery), Dreamstime (Jdazuelos,
Oknebulog, Swisshippo, Zakidesign), Getty Images (William F. Campbell/Timepix/Time & Life Pictures,
Central Press, Koichi Kamoshida, Latitudestock, Stocktrek, Peter Wilson), iStockphoto (Dean Bergmann,
Bart Everett, Alex Potemkin), Shutterstock (Ranga Yogeshwalka)

Library of Congress Cataloging-in-Publication Data

Bodden, Valerie.
Battleships / by Valerie Bodden.
Includes bibliographical references and index.
Summary: A fundamental exploration of battleships, including their size and firepower, history of
development, gun turrets and other features, and famous models from around the world.
ISBN 978-1-60818-124-7
1. Battleships—Juvenile literature. I. Title.
V815.B64 2011
623.825'2—dc22 2010053675

CPSIA: 112612 PO1620

4 6 8 9 7 5 3

BATTLESHIPS

Valerie Bodden

TABLE OF
contents

A huge ship sails through the ocean.

Fire blazes from the end of big guns on its

top deck. A loud boom echoes over the water.

This is a battleship!

Battleships once carried the biggest guns and the heaviest ARMOR of any warships. They were used to fight other battleships during wars. They could also shoot at airplanes and targets on land. Battleships could sail through the water at 24 to 38 miles (39-61 km) per hour.

Guns used to shoot

at airplanes are called

anti-aircraft guns

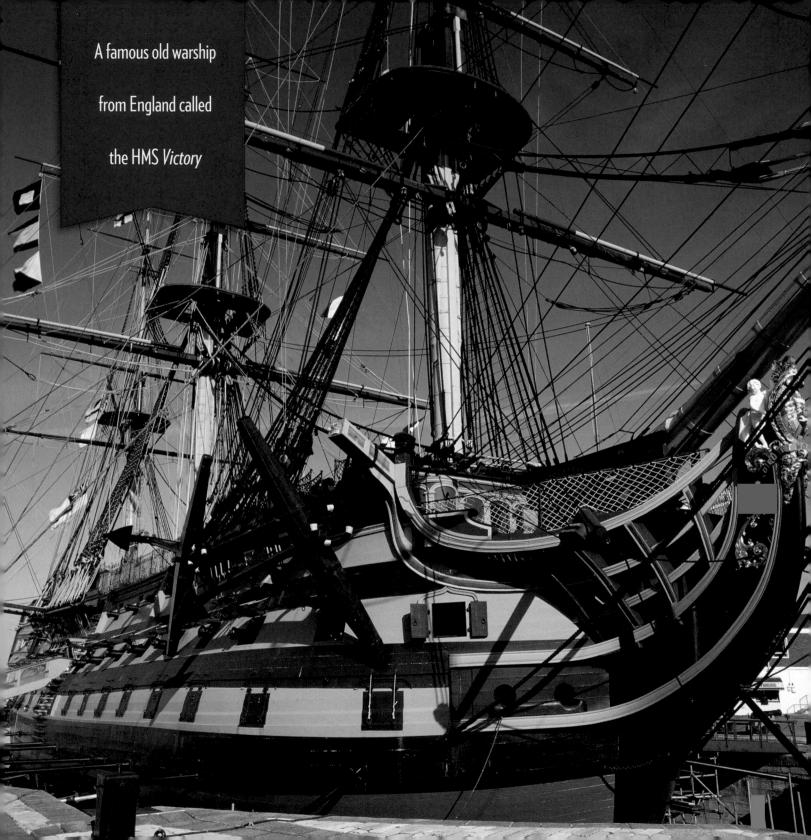

A famous old warship

from England called

the HMS *Victory*

The first large warships were built almost 500 years ago. They were wooden ships with sails. Later, battleships were made of strong metals and had powerful ENGINES. Between the 1940s and the 1970s, most countries got rid of their battleships. The United States used its battleships until 1991. Today, smaller, faster ships called CRUISERS and DESTROYERS have taken over many of the battleships' jobs.

The biggest battleships were more than 850 feet (259 m) long. That is longer than two football fields! They were about 100 feet (30.5 m) wide. Big propellers called screws moved battleships through the water.

Big battleships could
be more than
200 feet (61 m) tall

Views of a battleship

from the side (left)

and front (right)

Battleships had many decks, or levels. Some of the decks had living and eating areas. A battleship's top deck had a tall tower called the superstructure.

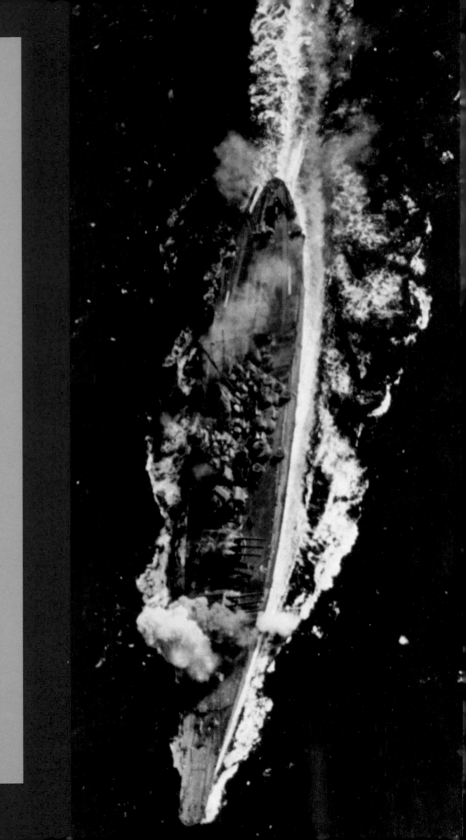

★ Famous Battleship ★
Yamato Class

COUNTRY

Japan

ENTERED SERVICE

1941

LENGTH

863 feet (263 m)

WIDTH

121 feet (37 m)

WEIGHT

62,315 tons (56,530 t)

FASTEST SPEED

31 miles (50 km) per hour

CREW

2,500

Yamato class battleships were the
heaviest battleships ever built.
Their huge guns were 18 inches
(46 cm) wide and could fire shells
up to 26 miles (42 km)!

A battleship's biggest guns were longer than school buses! The guns stuck out of TURRETS in groups of two or three. The turrets could turn the guns to shoot in different directions.

U.S. sailors standing

on a battleship deck

under gun turrets

A battleship captain controlled the ship from a room on the superstructure called the bridge. About 300 to 2,500 sailors worked on each battleship. They lived on the ship for months at a time.

Iowa Class

COUNTRY

United States

ENTERED SERVICE

1943

LENGTH

887 feet (270 m)

WIDTH

108 feet (33 m)

WEIGHT

57,450 tons (52,118 t)

FASTEST SPEED

38 miles (61 km) per hour

CREW

1,921

Iowa class battleships were the fastest battleships ever built. They were used in different wars for almost 50 years! Over time, they got new weapons such as MISSILES (*MIS-sulz*).

Battleship guns (top left);

shells (top right);

guns firing (bottom)

When a battleship went to war, sailors fired its guns. Some of the guns could fire SHELLS 26 miles (42 km). Battleships used in the 1990s could fire missiles more than 1,600 miles (2,575 km)!

Battleships also had smaller guns to help protect them from small warships. Their thick armor protected them from enemy attacks. It kept the battleships safe to fight another day!

Kirov Class

COUNTRY

Russia

ENTERED SERVICE

1980

LENGTH

827 feet (252 m)

WIDTH

94 feet (28.7 m)

WEIGHT

24,300 tons (22,045 t)

FASTEST SPEED

37 miles (60 km) per hour

CREW

710

Kirov class ships are large, heavy cruisers. They are not true battleships but are almost as big as the battleships of the past. They carry many different kinds of missiles.

GLOSSARY

armor—a layer of metal and other strong materials that covers a military vehicle and protects it from attacks

cruisers—warships that have less armor than battleships and are smaller and easier to steer; today most cruisers carry missiles that can hit targets far away

destroyers—warships that are smaller than cruisers; they are fast and easy to steer and can be used to attack submarines or to protect other ships

engines—machines that use energy to make things, such as cars or ships, move

missiles—exploding weapons that are pushed through the air by rockets to hit a target

shells—objects that are shot from a large gun and are filled with materials that can explode

turrets—parts of a ship that have armor and guns attached to them and can turn to point in different directions

INDEX

WEB SITES

Battleship New Jersey http://www.battleshipnewjersey.org/press_room/images.php Check out pictures of the battleship *New Jersey*.

Super Coloring: Military Coloring Pages http://www.supercoloring.com/pages/category/military/ Print and color pictures of all your favorite military machines.

READ MORE

Demarest, Chris. *Alpha, Bravo, Charlie: The Military Alphabet*. New York: Margaret K. McElderry Books, 2005.

O'Brien, Patrick. *The Great Ships*. New York: Walker & Company, 2001.